A BOOK TO BEGIN ON

Dinosaurs

Eunice Holsaert
Robert Gartland

HOLT, RINEHART AND WINSTON
CHICAGO   SAN FRANCISCO   NEW YORK

Library of Congress Catalog Card Number: 59-6245

ISBN 0–03–015646–7

Printed in the United States of America

Millions and millions of years ago, a little horn-faced dinosaur lay down on its back and died.

It lived and died long before there were any people on the earth.

Protoceratops

73110

Millions of years passed. The earth slowly shifted and changed.

The green, swampy land turned into dry desert.

The body of the little horn-faced dinosaur was hidden under the hot sands. It became a fossil.

Fossils are buried parts of animals or plants that have turned to stone.

A few years ago, some men went to the desert to hunt for fossils.

They found the clean, fossil bones of the little dinosaur.

The fossil hunters also found some dinosaur eggs that had turned to stone.

Inside a few of the eggs were the bones of horn-faced dinosaurs.

Protoceratop Babies

Probably, thousands of these little animals once lived in this desert.

These small dinosaurs were gentle plant-eaters, BUT...

Adult Protoceratops

They had many huge relatives who were not gentle.

Dinosaur means TERRIBLE LIZARD, and some dinosaurs were terrible indeed.

Where did these huge, terrible lizards come from?

In the far, far past, when our earth was very young, all living things made their homes in the sea.

No animals lived on the land.

Most of these first animals
looked like plants.

Slowly, the animals changed. Some grew teeth that helped them get food. Many grew stiff backbones that helped them swim faster.

They began to look less like plants and more like fish.

After another long while, some of the fish grew very large and fierce.

These giant fish, with huge teeth, gulped down weak, small fish by the hundreds.

Dinichthys

Some of the weaker fish began to change. The changes helped them get away from their enemies.

They grew lungs. Now they could breathe air.

Their enemies, without lungs, could not chase them to the top of the water.

A few of the air-breathing fish
began to grow short, weak legs.

They pulled their bodies on to
the swampy land.

At last they had left the sea.
They were safe from their enemies.

Diplocaulus

Eryops

Soon, many smooth-skinned animals like LONG FACE lived in the swamps.

Here they had few enemies, and plenty to eat.

Long Face could live on the land, or in the water.

But these land-water animals still laid their eggs in the water.

Their eggs were soft as jelly. They could not be left in the hot sun to hatch.

Their babies were called tadpoles. They did not have legs when they were born. They grew them later.

Tadpoles

Egg Case

Cotylosaur

At last an animal was born that could live its whole life on the land. This animal was a reptile.

OLDEST REPTILE lived on the land all the time. Instead of soft skin, it had hard scales. It moved quickly on strong legs.

Its eggs did not dry out. They hatched in the hot sun.

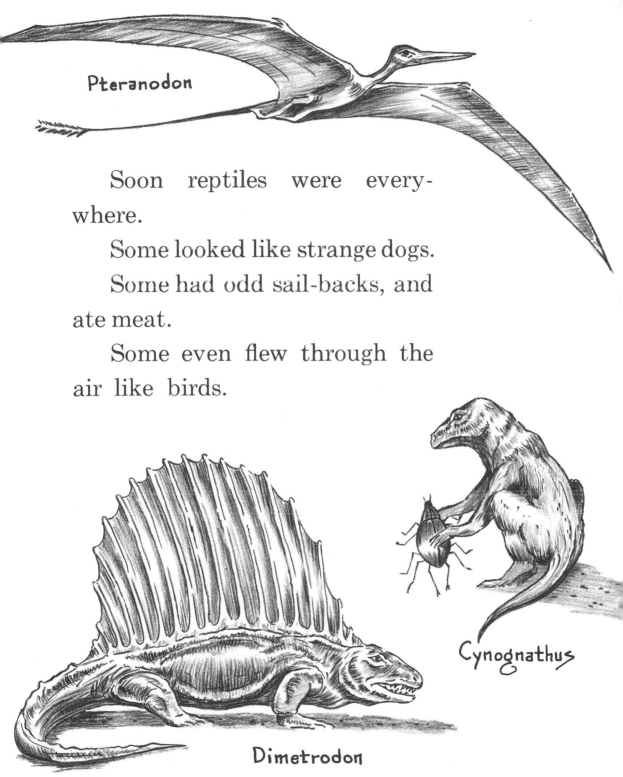

Pteranodon

Soon reptiles were every-where.

Some looked like strange dogs.

Some had odd sail-backs, and ate meat.

Some even flew through the air like birds.

Cynognathus

Dimetrodon

But the greatest of all the reptiles were the dinosaurs.

They were the strongest reptiles in the world, but they were stupid.

Even the largest dinosaurs had tiny brains.

Smaller animals with bigger brains could fool them.

For about 120 million years dinosaurs were lords of the earth.

During that long s-t-r-e-t-c-h of time many new shapes and sizes of dinosaurs were born.

Man has only been lord of the earth for a few million years.

He has not had time to change very much.

Man's life on earth is just a drop in the bucket of time.

It would barely cover the bottom of the bucket.

The time the dinosaurs spent on the earth would fill the bucket. drop by drop, year by year.

SMALLEST LIZARD was one of the early dinosaurs. It was a dainty little animal—about the size of a chicken.

BIRD ROBBER looked very much like Smallest Lizard but it was as tall as a man. It ran fast on its bird-like feet.

Ornitholestes

Allosaurus

HUNTING LIZARD was thirty-five feet long.

It could have eaten its lunch from the top of a house.

It was a fierce hunter. It ate meat.

We know that Hunting Lizard killed and ate the swamp dinosaurs, which were much larger than he.

Fossil hunters have found half-eaten swamp dinosaurs. These fossils had Hunting Lizard's teeth marks on them.

This huge fossil footprint was left by THUNDER LIZARD.

It was found in a Texas river bed.

Thunder Lizard was one of the largest dinosaurs. Its footsteps must have sounded like thunder as it plodded through the swamps.

This huge beast was a harm-
less plant-eater. It ate more in a
day than you eat in a year.

Brontosaurus

LARGEST LIZARD was as long as three busses. It was as heavy as six elephants.

Largest Lizard was the biggest animal that ever walked the earth. Only the great blue whale has ever grown larger.

Largest Lizard spent most of its time napping in a swamp. The water helped hold up its huge body.

Now it became cold and most
of the swamp plants died.

Many of the dinosaurs could
not find food.

Others died of the cold.

A few dinosaurs left the land
and went back to live in the sea.

Their legs turned into paddles
and flippers.

They were the terror of the
seas.

Plesiosaur

Later, when it was warm again, new kinds of dinosaurs were born.

TYRANT KING hunted everywhere. It was the most terrible dinosaur of them all.

Its huge jaws opened wider than you can stretch your arms.

It ate every living animal that it could find.

Tyrannosaurus

Desmatosuchus

Some of the plant-eating dinosaurs grew hard plates of bone on their bodies.

These odd bones helped protect them from Tyrant King.

They were as safe as knights in armor.

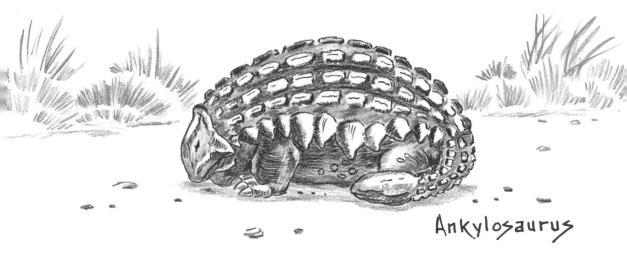

Ankylosaurus

ARMORED LIZARD curled up tight under its bony plates when Tyrant King came in sight.

It also had a big club of solid bone on the end of its tail.

This was useful for whacking smaller animals.

Stegosaurus

PLATE-BACK LIZARD was hard for Tyrant King to grab.

Plate-Back Lizard was also able to take care of itself in a strange way.

Its tiny brain could not manage its huge body.

So it grew a helping-brain, near its hips. This brain helped steer its back legs and its tail.

It worked like the back steering wheel of a long fire engine.

Other giant swamp lizards had helping brains, too.

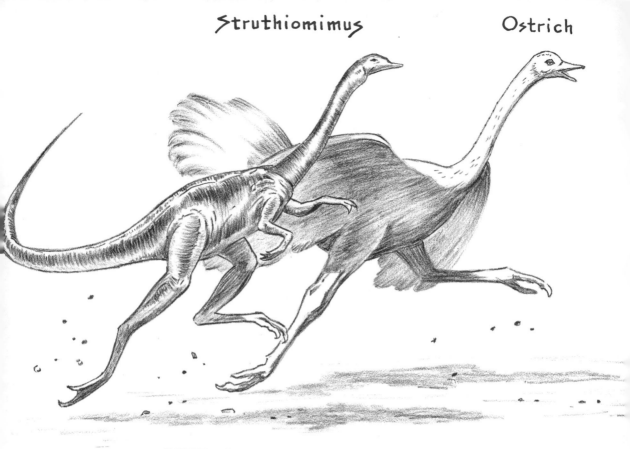

Struthiomimus   Ostrich

OSTRICH-LIKE DINOSAUR was a cousin of Tyrant King. But it was a gentle animal.

Its tiny head had no teeth. It had a beak like a bird.

It used its hands to pick fruit and crack eggs. It often hunted insects, too.

THREE-HORNED-FACE was one of the few dinosaurs that dared to fight Tyrant King.

Most of the time, Three-Horned-Face made no trouble. It wandered through the woods eating plants.

But it was not afraid to jab at Tyrant King with its horns.

Triceratops

Corythosaur

Among the last of the dino-saurs were the DUCK-BILL DINO-SAURS.

Most of them had rows, and rows, and rows of teeth inside their duck-like bills. They used their teeth to break off water plants.

These dinosaurs were good swimmers. They had webbed feet like ducks.

The Duck-Bill Dinosaurs sank under the water when they saw Tyrant King.

The one with a head like a deer could stay under water a long time. It kept air stored in its "horn."

Parasaurolophus

Now hard times came for all the dinosaurs.

Smart, small, furry animals stole the dinosaurs' eggs. Few dinosaurs were hatched.

Then, winter came to the earth. Now, even the mighty Tyrant King died.

Not one dinosaur lived in all the world.

Turtle

Today, there are just a few reptiles on earth to remind us of the Terrible Lizards that once ruled the world.

Crocodile

Tuatara

SOME FACTS TO REMEMBER

The word dinosaur means "terrible lizard." All dinosaurs were reptiles. Some ate plants. Some ate meat. Some dinosaurs were almost as big as a whale. A few were as small as a chicken. There are no dinosaurs alive today. But you can see their fossils in the museum.